CASTAWAY

Escaping the Island of Hopelessness

A book designed to deal with 21st Century isolation, loneliness, anxiety,

and depression

By A. Scott Miller

In cooperation with the Authorized Biography Company of

Hamilton, Ohio

Copyright 2010 by A. Scott Miller

All rights reserved. No portion of this book may be reproduced in any form without permission from the publisher, except for brief excerpts for educational purposes or review.

All Scripture quotations in this book are from the Kings James Version (KJV).

Published by:

Authorized Biography Company
480 Dexter Court
Hamilton, Ohio 45013
To order more books, call (513) 544-4266.

Dedication

To Helen Louise Anderson Miller: whom I affectionately called "Mamaw" for forty years. Her old fashioned philosophy on life kept her strong and stable. With all of life's ups and downs, she always viewed herself as a soldier and a servant of the Lord. She ever taught us to "just keep on marching."

Contents

Acknowledgments		9
Preface		11
Introduction		15
Plank 1:	Recognize you don't know everything	29
Plank 2:	Relax. Choose to believe that God knows everything and He can do anything	39
Plank 3:	Repent of your sins; stop giving yourself the right to a pity party.	49
Plank 4:	React humbly. Become the servant of God. Pray and minister to others.	59
Plank 5:	Resolve to be patient. Let God be God. You never know what time or the tide will bring in.	69
Plank 6:	Receive advice and resources. Let others help you.	77
Plank 7:	Resist negativism and make a new life out of what the Lord gives you.	93
Afterword		112
Endnotes		114

Acknowledgments

There are several people to whom I must render heartfelt thanks. I appreciate all the time and energy you spent painstakingly going through the first drafts of this book. To Martin and Norma Hall, Ernie and Emma Warren, Charlie Schweizer, Donna Miller, Dianna McCleese, Pastor David Schenk and Pastor Barry Wilson: thank you for your contributions in editing Castaway. I am most grateful.

To Fantacy Bryant (www.fantacybryantphotography.com), I appreciate the keen eye that you have for photography. Thank you for your illustrations throughout this book. I also want to thank my volunteer models: Charlie Schweizer, Dave and Etta Proffitt, Taylor Miller, Lane Bryant, Laura Powers and Bethani Miller.

To Chris Miller, Wayne Rogers and Impact Direct Marketing: Thank you for the design of the cover and for always answering the phone when we called with technical issues.

To my wife, Jodi, who continually keeps me on track, who sacrificed hours to type, edit and format this book. Thank you, doll. You know better than anyone that, literally, I could not have completed this book without you.

To my church family, thank you for allowing me the time to put my thoughts down on paper in an effort to help others escape their Island of Hopelessness.

Preface

Since the terrorist attacks of September 11, 2001, our country has been in a hazy fog. The 21st century started off tragically and has only gotten worse. As a nation, we have dealt with one battle after another. We have sloshed through and slugged it out with just about every conceivable problem: whether it be the Iraq war, Hurricane Katrina, gas hikes, Wall Street meltdown, housing market collapse, or the current 2009 devastating recession. As individuals we have lost our homes and our jobs, our retirement has been cut in half, our families struggle to stay together, and we live with the fear of what tomorrow will bring.

Life, at this moment in time, with all its modern conveniences, seems to be redefining mankind's purpose, his happiness, values, hopes and dreams. We are left wondering "What am I supposed to do? What am I to crave and desire? What am I supposed to enjoy? From what am I supposed to abstain? Whom should I trust? Who can really help me? Why should I stay alive? Why should I keep going? Why should I stay with my spouse? Why am I here? How do I get satisfaction and fulfillment out of life?" Bottom line… "How am I to live?"

Many people think that isolation, loneliness, anxiety, and depression are modern day issues. But back when man first stepped foot on this planet, he struggled with depression. Thousands of years ago, we, as men and women, felt lonely and isolated. We felt like no one could understand our worry, fear, and constant anxiety. Needless to say, mankind has been battling the island of hopelessness for a long time.

But our Creator has not left us without a way of escape. Through the ancient scriptures, He has given us example after example of men and women who completely bottomed out. Because of their circumstances, people couldn't go on or they didn't even want to go on. Yet, God gave them the materials, tools, and the skills to build a raft; escape the Island of Hopelessness; and return back home to happiness, fulfillment, peace, and purpose. But let me be frank and honest with you. Some made it…others did not.

The choice will be yours as always- to obey God or disobey God. God has given us this freedom but unfortunately with this freedom comes consequences. As the Lord asked a crippled man in the Gospel of John, "Wilt thou be made whole?", the choice is yours. I can promise you that God wants you to know His peace and joy. The old saying for salvation also applies here: "God voted for you. Satan voted against you. You cast the deciding vote."

You're reading this book for one of two reasons: one, you desperately want help, or two, you want guidance on how to help someone else. The individuals who are on the Island of Hopelessness feel like something is looming over them. They're under a constant strain. Day and night, they get no relief. The anxiety of their situation is just killing them. There is a lot of truth in that statement.

Scientists and medical students have been doing experiments on rats and mice for many decades. They have discovered that when rats are taken out of their normal environment and subjected to extreme temperatures- cold or hot, restricted from exercise, frustrated constantly at every turn of life, stressed out even by loud noise or extreme silence, lethal health issues pop up: blood pressure soars, blood sugar increases, fats from the body are dumped into the blood and deposited along artery walls of the heart, and peptic ulcers develop. Take a mouse and a cat and put them in two cages side by side. Because the cat is continually looming over the mouse, that mouse will eventually die of anxiety.

Are humans any different? Can you put your finger on what dark cloud is ever hovering over you? With the principles and lessons laid out for us in the book of Job, I hope to remove that dark cloud.

It is my hope and prayer that Castaway brings you back to the place at which you will truly soar in the sky and enjoy life once again.

–A. Scott Miller

Introduction

Samantha walked back to the pastor's office. She paused just for a moment before she knocked on the half-closed door. She had twin daughters and had been married to her husband for fourteen years. The Wednesday night service had ended minutes ago. She knocked.

"Come in," she heard from the other side of the door.

"Pastor, could I talk with you for just a minute?"

"Why sure, Samantha. Come on in. Have a seat."

Pastor Waltz was almost sixty now and had been with this church for almost eighteen years. He directed Samantha over to a couple of couches he had in his office for meetings and counseling sessions. As they sat down, the pastor noticed that Samantha's arms and forehead had scabs on them and were covered by some sort of white lotion.

"Samantha, what is all over your arms and head?"

"Oh, I honestly don't know, and the doctors don't know either. It's some kind of skin disease, an allergic reaction to something, or quite possibly something to do with my nerves. I just itch all the time. The lotion is supposed to help."

"Oh, my goodness, how long have you been itching?"

"About two weeks," Samantha said, as she scratched her left arm.

"Well, I am so sorry. Is it getting any better?" asked Pastor Waltz.

"No, I can't say that it is. I go back to the doctor next week if it gets worse."

"Well, besides that, how have you been?"

"Pastor, I'm afraid not very well. Aaron left me last week and he took our girls with him."

The pastor had to stop and think for a minute about what Samantha had just said. He was trying to picture in his mind what Aaron looked like. Aaron didn't come to church, and from what Pastor Waltz could remember, he was not a Christian, or at least he didn't act like one. The girls, on the other hand, had come to the church nearly their whole lives, up to the last year when their sports lives really started to take off. Then they missed quite often. Their dad was their basketball coach and worked the girls hard on the weekends.

"What happened?" asked Pastor Waltz.

"Aaron says he just doesn't love me anymore and that we were really too young to even know what love was when we got married. We've been having problems for the last couple of years, so it didn't come as too much of a surprise. But he took the girls."

"What do the girls have to say about this?"

"Well, they don't like it but he's their coach. They said when they don't have practice or games they'll come to see me. Pastor, it's just awful."

Samantha began to cry. Pastor Waltz got up and grabbed a box of tissues from behind his desk. Samantha wiped her eyes and then balled up the tissue in her hand.

"Pastor, I'm in our four-bedroom house, all alone. I can't afford it. My boss is Aaron's dad. So I don't know how much longer I'll have my job. Pastor, I just feel like I've lost everything. I've lost my husband, I've lost my children, I've lost my health, I've lost my home, and now I've lost my job. What am I going to do?"

As she spoke, her head went down into her hands and she began to sob. The office was quiet for what felt like an eternity. Pastor Waltz felt numb. One half of him wanted to get up and find Aaron and knock some sense into him. The other half was trying to figure out what to say to comfort Samantha, to give her the advice she needed. But what does one say to the person who's lost all the comforts of life? This young lady, just in her early thirties, was dealing with health issues, rejection, worthlessness, hopelessness, purposelessness, loneliness and more than likely, poverty. No home, no family, no money, no physical comforts, no love and no perceivable future....

THE STORY OF JOB

Scholars tell us that the oldest book in the Bible is Job. Before Abraham, Moses, or even Noah, Job lived. The story of Job is quite simple. He lost everything. What Samantha is going through has happened before.

I believe it might be helpful to discuss depression and its causes before we talk about Job and his situation. Depression is defined in the Webster's Dictionary as "a state of feeling sad: a psychoneurotic or psychotic disorder marked especially by sadness, inactivity, difficulty in thinking and concentration, a significant increase or decrease in appetite and time spent sleeping, feelings of dejection and hopelessness, and sometimes suicidal tendencies."

Depression comes as a result of losing something. It is a sadness, uncontrollable moodiness, unexplainable fatigue, anger, and a lack of motivation that camps out in someone's life. If you suffer with it, you agree with Psalm 55:6: "And I said, Oh that I had wings like a dove! For then would I fly away, and be at rest." You want to fly away. You want to get in a car and just drive as far as you can from your problems. A significant loss, for instance, could be a loss of a job, loss of a spouse, loss of a friendship, loss of a home, loss of money, or loss of a loved one.

These all can cause us to grieve and hurt, but we must not stop the list there.

Many more losses come in people's lives everyday. They fall under the radar of consciousness. We tend to overlook them or dismiss them. They are difficult to put your finger on, but they are there. They, too, will cause you to slump, sigh, and regret life. They will cause you to search for forbidden fruit in hopes of finding a new spark to light the fire of your heart again. These losses are more subtle:

- *A loss of a dream: you've been saving and planning to retire to Florida for the last ten years. The stock market crashes and you lose half your money. All your desires and hopes were directed to that plan. You feel deflated, unmotivated, and angry. Now what are you going to do?*
- *How about a loss of respect for a mentor? You looked up to and admired this person for a long time. You wanted to be just like him. Morally he stumbled and fell. Scandal surrounds his life, and you are left confused. Whom can you trust?*
- *Still another could be a loss of a burden. You've been caring for a sick loved one. Twice, everyday, you stop in to check on him/her and arrange the meals and medicine. Then he/she passes away. After the funeral you enjoy the freedom and relief, but then it hits you like a ton of bricks: He/she is gone, never to come back again. For years, that's what balanced you and gave you stability. It has restricted your time, but now you're left with the question, "Why am I here?"*

- *Unfortunately, there are also cruel and wicked people in this world who victimize others for their own pleasure. Loss of innocence is most damaging. You painted the world in beautiful pastel colors of pink, yellow, and violet. People were fun, life was good, and then it happened. You were tricked, robbed, duped, or even raped. Now the world is black and gray. Why should you stay alive?*
- *A loss many Hollywood actors, rock stars, and politicians face is a loss of resistance. They've struggled and fought to make it to the top. Their careers can go no further. They're at the height of their game. But now that life is easy, their struggles have ceased, and they have their goals in hand; they find the top of the mountain is not all that great. They ask, "Is this all there is?"*

Job lost his family, his wealth, and his health. He literally got to the place, as so many have when depression strikes, where he said, "I'd rather be dead than go through this." Job 10:1 says, *"My soul is weary of my life..."* It should be noted that often times isolation, loneliness, anxiety, and depression come into our lives because of something we have done, and we must take responsibility for it. We made a choice and WHAM...the consequences hit, and they are dire.

- *A decision we made results in our own isolation, and we end up cut off from a spouse or from other people because of something stupid we said or did.*

- *We neglect our own children for years, and they grow up, and because we had no time for them when they were young, now they have no time for us. We end up lonely in our middle age, and we have no intimate bonds with our adult children.*
- *We decide after high school to join the working world. It's time to make some cash. Older mentors in our lives tell us to plan out a career, find something that interests us or that we'd love to do. We ignore their advice, skip college, abandon trade school, and get a job. At eighteen-years-old, we're making good money. But after ten years of grinding toil, we end up feeling empty. We feel like we're wasting away. But at age twenty-eight, there are kids, a spouse, a home mortgage, a car payment and every other conceivable bill under the sun....Who has time to plan life out now?*

Those decisions lead us to depression and the Island of Hopelessness. We can change, but the price will be extremely high...move to a smaller house, resort to junk cars, cut all non-critical spending, take a part-time job, and go back to school. Is it worth it? If you want off the Island of Hopelessness, it is. But in the circumstance of Job, his sadness came through no fault of his own. He did not cause it. All these things just happened. He lost everything. He couldn't have stopped it if he tried.

Dr. Charles Brown tells a story in the August 2008 issue of "The Landmark Anchor" magazine. (1) He says that years ago he was deer hunting in Brown County, Indiana. It was a beautiful autumn day and the valley he was walking through was carpeted by leaves. There was not much brush, so the view was clear. As he was strolling through the woods, something made him look down. He stopped. Not three feet in front of him was a circular hole where an old well used to be. Another step or two and he would have gone in. He laid down his gun and crept to the edge. The hole was about four feet wide and the drop to the black inky water was about six feet down. If he had fallen in, who knows if he would have been able to get out.

Life, unfortunately, is like that at times. We are walking along, enjoying the beauty, our mind focused on something else, and splash! We fall into a hole that shouldn't have been there. Yes, maybe we can avoid it by watching and being more careful, but what if some boards had been placed over the hole and after years of aging are weak. Leaves cover the hole. You casually walk along cautious and alert, doing everything right, and splash! You go into the water anyway. That's what happened to Job. Consequently he's sloshing around in depression.

To recap what happened to Job, we must look back to the book that bears his name, Job, chapters one and two. The Scriptures point out that Satan and God had a conversation. And to Job's dismay it was about him. Look at that passage once again.

Job 1:6-22 says, *"Now there was a day when the sons of God came to present themselves before the Lord, and Satan came also among them. And the Lord said unto Satan, Whence comest thou? Then Satan answered the Lord, and said, From going to and fro in the earth, and from walking up and down in it. And the Lord said unto Satan, Hast thou considered my servant, Job, that there is none like him in the earth, a perfect and an upright man, one that feareth God, and escheweth evil? Then Satan answered the Lord, and said, Doth Job fear God for nought? Hast not thou made a hedge about him, and about his house, and about all that he hath on every side? Thou hast blessed the work of his hands, and his substance is increased in the land. But put forth thine hand now, and touch all that he hath, and he will curse thee to thy face. And the Lord said unto Satan, Behold, all that he hath is in thy power; only upon himself put not forth thine hands. So Satan went forth from the presence of the Lord.*

And there was a day when his sons and his daughters were eating and drinking wine in their eldest brother's house. And there came a messenger unto Job, and said, The oxen were plowing, and the asses feeding beside them: And the Sabeans fell upon them, and took them away; yea, they have slain the servants with the edge of the sword; and I only am escaped alone to tell thee. While he was yet speaking, there came also another, and said, The fire of God is fallen from heaven, and hath burned up the sheep, and the servants, and consumed them; and I only am escaped alone to tell thee. While he was yet speaking, there came also another, and said, The Chaldeans made out three bands, and fell upon the camels, and have carried them away, yea, and slain the servants with the edge of the sword; and I only am escaped alone to tell thee. While he was yet speaking, there came also another, and said, Thy sons and thy daughters were eating and drinking wine in their eldest brother's house: And, behold, there came a great wind from the wilderness, and smote the four corners of the house, and it fell upon the young men, and they are dead; and I only am escaped alone to tell thee. Then Job arose, and rent his mantle, and shaved his head, and fell down upon the ground, and worshiped. And said, Naked came I out of my mother's womb, and naked shall I return thither: the Lord gave, and the Lord hath taken away; blessed be the name of the Lord. In all this Job sinned not, nor charged God foolishly."

Job 2:1-7 says, *"Again there was a day when the sons of God came to present themselves before the Lord, and Satan came also among them to present himself before the Lord. And the Lord said unto Satan, From whence comest thou? And Satan answered the Lord, and said, From going to and fro in the earth, and from walking up and down in it.*

And the Lord said unto Satan, Hast thou considered my servant Job, that there is none like him in the earth, a perfect and an upright man, one that feareth God, and escheweth evil? And still he holdeth fast his integrity, although thou movedst me against him, to destroy him without cause. And Satan answered the Lord, and said, Skin for skin, yea, all that a man hath will he give for his life. But put forth thine hand now, and touch his bone and his flesh, and he will curse thee to thy face. And the Lord said unto Satan, Behold, he is in thine hand; but save his life. So went Satan forth from the presence of the Lord, and smote Job with sore boils from the sole of his foot unto his crown."

Job didn't know why all this was happening to him. He was beyond miserable. In fact, he gives us his thought in the key verse to this whole tragedy in Job 3:25, *"For the thing which I greatly feared is come upon me, and that which I was afraid of is come unto me."* Imagine the worst thing that can happen to you, the worst thing you can think of. Job says that's what "came upon me."

If you are reading this book right now, and you are miserable, you've lost your zeal for life, you are on the Island of Hopelessness...then, you're in good company. Job lost everything...health, wealth, and family. He, too, sat on the same deserted island. He, too, watched the waves crash in with no hope of getting off.

Water surrounded him. Sand, palm trees, and rocks were his only friends. Isolation and loneliness gripped his soul. He sat alone in his misery because no one understood the pain he was undergoing. No one understood the burden he was carrying. Sure, Job had people around him: a spouse, servants, and friends. But no one understood his personal anguish and suffering just like your friends don't understand your anguish and suffering.

But Job got off the island. And so can you. Your only hope is to build a raft for yourself. No one is coming to rescue you. No helicopters, planes, or boats will venture your way. No one will swoop in to carry you home. You will have to take full responsibility. By working hard and by God's grace you will get off this Island of Hopelessness and sail back to civilization.

Imagine, if you will, that this is a practical guide to raft making. It is not just theories and pleasantries. If fiercely practiced and concretely put into place in your life, you will paddle away from the island. But if you just read this "how-to" manual and never put its principles into place, you will forever sit on the beach.

Let us begin to gather the wood and make our planks. These planks come straight from ancient scriptures; not from the latest pop psychology, but from the ultimate Counselor, God.

"Where are the answers?"

Plank One:

Recognize you don't know everything

"Then the Lord answered Job out of the whirlwind, and said, Who is this that darkeneth counsel by words without knowledge?" Job 38:1-2

    For the last thirty-five chapters, Job, his associates, friends and counselors have tried to figure out what was wrong. Why did all this happen? Why did Job lose everything? What should he do now? They have given their opinions and exchanged philosophies. They have talked and talked trying to come up with their best conclusions. Finally God answers and the first thing he says is "You don't know everything. You and your friends don't have a clue. You don't have the full story." Notice the last phrase of verse two: You are talking "without knowledge." Today young people might say "You don't know Jack." As human beings on planet earth, we must come to grips with the idea that some things are hidden from our eyes. God doesn't let us in on everything. A concrete example of this is found in Daniel 12:4, 8, 9. *"But thou, O Daniel, shut up the words, and seal the book, even to the time of the end..."* Verse eight says, *"And I heard, but I understood not: then said I, O my Lord, what shall be the end of these things? And he said, Go thy way, Daniel: for the words are closed up and sealed till the time of the end."*

"Daniel, you don't need to know. This is just for God and His angels." Another example is given in Revelation 10:4. *"And when the seven thunders had uttered their voices, I was about to write: and I heard a voice from heaven saying unto me, Seal up those things which the seven thunders uttered, and write them not."* God did not want John the Apostle to reveal what was uttered.

As castaways on the Island of Hopelessness, we must get comfortable with the idea that some of our questions will not be answered until we get to heaven. Why did I lose everything? All the comforts of life are gone. Why, God, why? Why did you take my loved one? Why did I lose all my earthly possessions? Why did I lose my job? Why did my dream die? Why is my body struck with this disease? This first plank on your raft is that you don't know everything. You don't know the whole story.

We live in a modern society that prides itself on information with twenty-four hours of cable TV news, the internet, and just about anything we need to know is at our finger tips. We don't like not knowing something. But when you think about it, we really don't know much. God goes on to ask Job several questions to prove that Job doesn't know everything. In fact, when God's done, He's proven Job really has a lot to learn. By just taking a quick glance through God's response to Job, we note several thought-provoking questions.

Look at Job 38:4. *"Where wast thou when I laid the foundations of the earth?"* Look at verse seven, *"When the morning stars sang together and all the sons of God shouted for joy?"* God is asking Job, "When I created the earth and the angels sang afterwards, were you there?" How about this one, Job? Verse twelve: *"Hast thou commanded the morning since thy days?..."* Job, do you make the sun come up everyday? The whole chapter is a series of unfathomable truths. I like verse thirty-one, *"Canst thou bind the sweet influences of Pleiades or loose the bands of Orion?"* Job, can you grab hold of the constellations? Can you reach the stars of the sky? Can you hold them in place?

Modern science, still to this day, struggles with the mysteries of the dinosaurs, but not God. He knows all about them. God says in Job

40:15-19, *"Behold now behemoth, which I made with thee; he eateth grass as an ox. Lo now, his strength is in his loins, and his force is in the navel of his belly."* God also points out that Job is very limited to what he knows about the giants of the sea. Job 41:1 says, *"Canst thou draw out leviathan with a hook? Or his tongue with a cord which thou lettest down?"* Job, you don't know much about creation, astronomy, geology, or even paleontology. And Job, you don't know the whole story behind your life. Job, you don't know everything. You couldn't comprehend it if you did. The first thing you must come to grips with is: there are some things you'll never understand. Stop beating yourself up and everybody else around you in trying to answer the question of "why?"

Stop and visualize yourself on a deserted island. You're on the beach. The sun is beating down upon you. As the waves crash around you, come to the conclusion: sometimes we just can't have our answer on this side of Heaven. It's all right because besides not understanding the circumstance, situation, and problem you're going through, there's a whole lot out there you don't understand.

Back in 2001, the entire nation was devastated. The worst attack on American soil had occurred. The events of 9/11 opened America's eyes to unexpected pain and suffering. A lot of finger-pointing began. Who was to blame? As a nation and a group, we all eventually pointed to God. "How could You let this happen? Why did You let this happen?" We were baffled. We didn't understand. Our questions were unanswered. But while the country dealt with massive problems, our family dealt with personal tragedy. We, too, were left wondering "Why?"

My mother married a wonderful man named Jerry back in 1987. It seemed like a match made in heaven. Jerry's first wife had passed away from cancer on Christmas morning in 1986. My soon-to-be two step sisters were left without their mother. Jerry and my mother married nine months later, and a new home was established.

Things were moving right along. The kids got married, grandkids began to be born…we were just one big happy family. Jerry had a good job. He was a construction supervisor. He poured his life into others, unselfishly, teaching Sunday School and Junior Church almost every Sunday morning for twenty years. Jerry never met a stranger. He was friendly, outgoing, and just one of the "good guys of life." Jerry and my mom were making plans for the empty-nest life. He loved golden oldies and southern gospel music and could fix a mean batch of biscuits and gravy. His construction company loved him, his church loved him, his friends loved him, the Junior Church kids loved him, his family loved him, and his wife loved him. But Jerry died at age 49.

In November, the day before Thanksgiving, we found out Jerry had cancer. He walked his daughter down the aisle a couple of weeks later on December 8th. He smiled from ear to ear, although he was in a lot of pain. He was not going to be a distraction at his daughter's wedding. An IV full of medicine was attached to him. He hid it as best he could. Two weeks after the wedding, on December 22nd, we got the call that we needed to come to the hospital quickly. When we arrived, we were told "He's gone". Not one month had gone by since we had been told that he had cancer. We were left with questions like, "Why? God, with all the dirty, idiotic, cruel, and selfish people on planet Earth, why would you take Jerry? He was truly instrumental in people's lives. He was kind, gentle, loving, and unselfish. With a long life ahead of him, to help Your cause, to teach children the Bible, God, why would You allow him to die?" He was a valuable piece of society in so many ways. As a family, we had to admit "God, this does not make any sense."

The answer never came. And to be honest with you, it probably never will. The answer will come one day in Heaven. Our family is not bitter. We are not mad at God. We accept His decisions. We may not like them, but we trust Him.

This first plank we put down on the beach, upon which we will add the others, is: We don't know the whole story. The big picture of *why* and *how* has not yet been revealed to us.

Slow down right now and pause for just a moment. What are you personally going through? It's driving you crazy, isn't it? You're trying to figure out: Why? How? Part of your anxiety is tied to these complex questions. You might not ever find out on this side of Heaven why your husband or wife just snapped and left you, why the accident happened, or why your loved one was struck with a terrible disease. Would it change the outcome if you did? Stop trying to figure out why, and just start living. We don't have to know everything. But it's okay; we will find out later.

For now…Plank One…"We simply don't know everything."

Raft Building Questions:
Plank One

1. As Job struggles with his present circumstances in losing everything, battling anxiety, and trying to understand why it all happened, what is the first thing God says to him in Job 38:1-2?

2. What is your most heartrending, life-stopping question? Write it down below. Be specific.

3. Are you alright with having some of your questions answered in Heaven?

4. What is the main lesson you take away from Plank One?

"Bitterness…but whose fault is it?"

Plank Two:

Relax. Choose to believe that God knows everything, and He can do anything.

"Then Job answered the Lord, and said, I know that thou canst do every thing, and that no thought can be withholden from thee." Job 42:1-2

The flip side of our not knowing everything and being very limited in what we can do is that God does know everything. He is absolutely sovereign and omniscient. Because of His omnipotence, He can do anything. Now little arguments come up such as, "Can God make a rock He can't pick up?" or a catchy phrase such as, "God does not know another way for you to go to Heaven besides accepting His Son as your personal Savior." We can come up with all kinds of witty questions and phrases, but the hard core, basic fact that we must get through our thick skulls is this: God is totally sovereign. God knows all, He sees all, and He can do all.

When you are on the Island of Hopelessness, it's nice to know that your universe is not spiraling out of control. God has everything covered. One television series every family across our great land can watch together is America's Funniest Home Videos. A classic circumstance captured over and over again, by many different families, is sled riding. It seems at least once during a show, you'll see a clip of a kid, parent, or even a grandparent who is careening, at mach four, down some hill, running into a tree, car, mailbox, or even the person holding the camera. We all laugh because most Americans have been there before- on a sled, out of control, heading right for "who knows what!"

At times, on the Island of Hopelessness, we feel our lives are out of control. "Who's driving this stupid thing anyway?" We can't turn; we can't stop. We can only hang on. But even though we feel as if our lives are hopelessly given to chance, we must never lose sight of this: God is in control.

Dr. James Dobson has helped millions of people all across the world. Years ago, he wrote a book entitled *"When God Doesn't Make Sense."* In that book, he shares one of the most tragic times of his life. He writes,

"I recall today that tragic time in 1987 when my four friends were killed in a private plane crash. We had been together the

night before and I had prayed for their safety on the journey home. They took off early the next morning on their way to Dallas, but never made it. I can never forget that telephone call indicating the wreckage that had been found in a remote canyon- but there were no survivors! I loved those men like brothers and I was staggered by their loss. I was asked by the four families to speak briefly at the funeral. The untimely deaths, of such vibrant and deeply loved men, seemed to scream for an explanation. Where was God in their passing? Why did He let this happen? Why would He take such godly men from their families and leave them reeling in grief and pain? There were no answers to these agonizing questions, and I did not try to produce them. But I did say that God had not lost control of their lives and that He wanted us to trust Him when nothing made sense. His presence was very near. As we exited the sanctuary that day, I stood by with loved ones and friends who had gathered to say goodbye. Suddenly, someone pointed to the sky and exclaimed, "Look at that!" Suspended directly above the steeple, was a small rainbow in the shape of a smile. There had been no precipitation that day and no more than a few fleecy clouds, yet this beautiful little rainbow appeared above the church. We learned later that it had been hovering there most of the funeral. It was as though the Lord was saying to the grieving wives and children, "Be at peace. Your men are with Me and all is well. I know you don't understand, but I want you to trust Me. I'm going to take care of you and this rainbow is a sign to remember."

Satan is only able to attack the faithful, born again Christian when God allows him. The question that notoriously pops up is "Why does He (God) ever allow Satan to attack?" Simply…as someone once said, "A faith that can't be tested, can't be trusted." We grow in the valleys of our lives. As we struggle, we look up to the sky for help. "God, where are You? Help me!" we clamor. Ahhh…now we get it. As we struggle through our circumstances, we get stronger.

Think of a caterpillar. As he is crawling around, he wonders what it would be like to fly. Then one day nature calls, and he builds a cocoon around himself. He is isolated from the world. He and God struggle alone on the inside; then, eventually part of his cocoon splits. Daylight comes bursting through but he is still trapped. His body is still changing as he squirms to loosen himself of his prison. His body grows stronger and a metamorphosis is taking place. After several grueling hours of being in agony, pain and near death, there is a transformation.

The caterpillar has changed into a beautiful butterfly, flying and soaring to new heights he never dreamed he could.

What made that possible? The isolated, lonely prison, which he called a cocoon, was, in fact, his ticket to a glorious future. Scientists who study these beautiful creatures will tell you the struggle is absolutely necessary. Say, for instance, if you were to take that cocoon when it first splits open, you see the pupa…caterpillar…then the butterfly struggle to get out. Very gently you cut open the rest of the cocoon to help. The butterfly squirms out and flops around on the ground, unable to fly because it is only half formed. It isn't ready. Part of its metamorphosis is the struggle. I've heard it phrased like this: "Adversity is God's University." Part of the butterfly's eventual state can come only through its pain, suffering, near death, isolation, and anxious struggle.

You're on the Island of Hopelessness for a reason. It is not God's intention for you to stay there. Part of who you are to become can only happen in pain and suffering. Therefore, struggle, fight, move, and squirm until that cocoon breaks. Then continue to battle. Don't give up. As daylight bursts through and you see the light at the end of the tunnel, grind away, stay focused on God's ultimate purpose for your life. Twist and turn until He says you're ready, then soar with Him in the sky as a beautiful butterfly. Let your mind meditate on the biblical fact that God knows all, sees all, and can do all things. Just because your life seems like it is out of sorts, it's not. It's not out of control. As a born-again Christian, you're right where you're supposed to be. Could God gently cut up your cocoon and release you from your Island of Hopelessness? Sure, He can do anything. But should He? Do you just want relief, or do you want the best life God has to offer?

Someone coined the phrase: "When you can't see God's hand, trust His heart." This is so often true. We don't understand God, but we must know He wants the best for us. Just like we want the best for our own children. Trust me, it's not the first time man didn't understand his Creator. Isaiah 55:8-9 says, *"For my thoughts are not your thoughts, neither are your ways my ways, saith the Lord. For as the heavens are higher than the earth, so are my ways higher than your ways, and my thoughts than your thoughts."* The same God who created the stars above, created you. The same God who makes the sun come up every morning, created you. He loves you and adores you. In fact, He says in Jeremiah 29:11, *"For I know the thoughts that I think toward you, saith the Lord, thoughts of peace, and not of evil, to give you an expected end."* The God of Heaven has a particular destiny for each of us. Sometimes that destiny can only come from being on the Island of Hopelessness. Be diligent and gather up your wood for your planks.

Plank One: "Recognize you don't know everything." Then go back and gather your wood for Plank Two: "Relax. Choose to believe that God knows everything and can do anything."

Could He bring you out of the state of depression? Sure. Should He? Not if you want what is best for Him and you. C.S. Lewis often said something like this, "God whispers in our happiness but shouts in our pain." We grow very little as believers on the top of the mountain. We grow immensely on the valley floor where the only thing we can do is hit our knees and look up and pray, "God help me." I promise you that He can, and He will when the time is right. The problem is not His ability; He can do anything. But what is best for you? Truly, right now, acknowledge God. Choose to believe that "God knows everything and can do anything. I need to put Plank Two down and relax."

Raft Building Questions:
Plank Two

1.   Write the definition of three words:

Omniscient:

Omnipotent:

Sovereign:

2. Do you believe your world is spinning out of control or that it is ultimately in God's capable hands?

3. In your own words, write what Jeremiah 29:11 means to you?

4. What is the main lesson you take away from Plank Two?

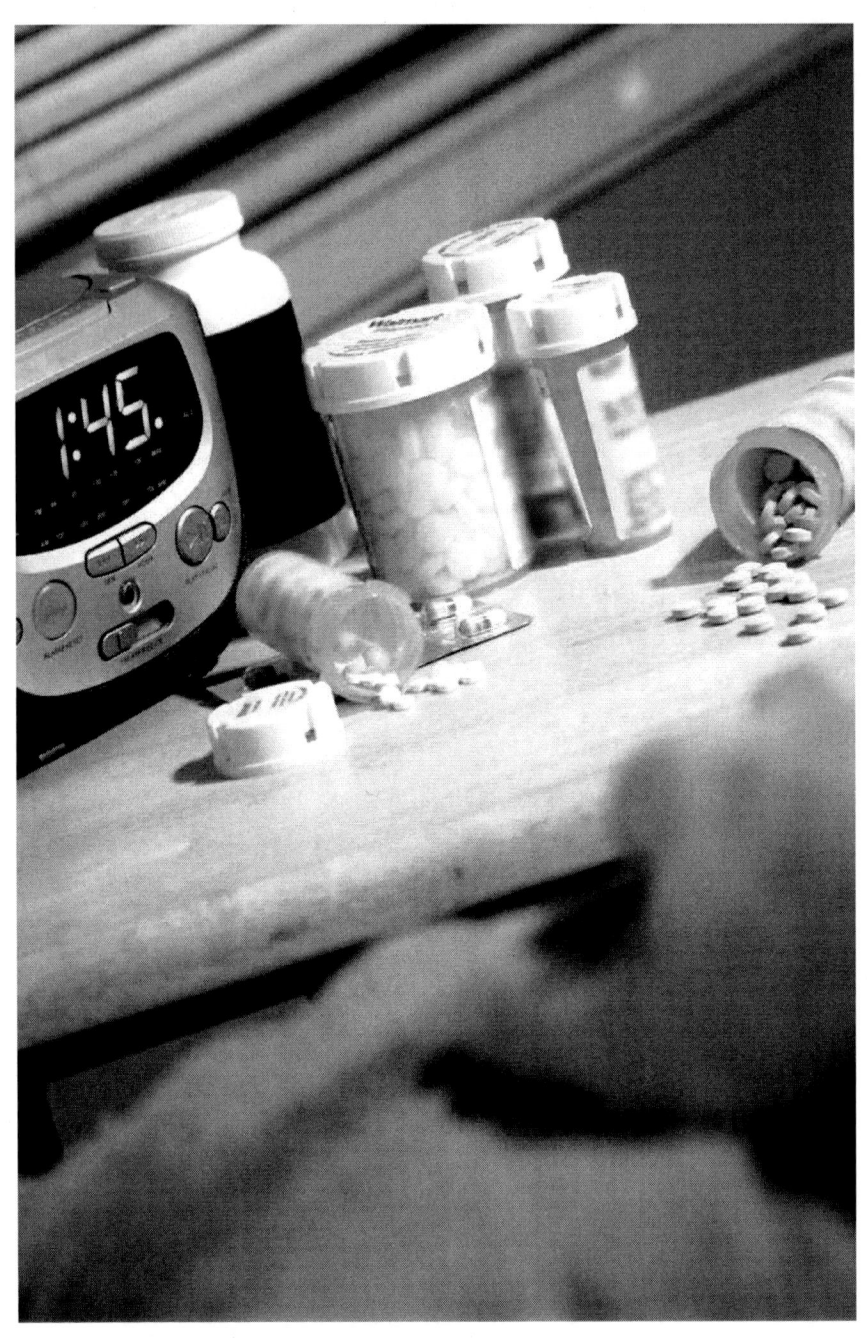

"Is this numbing the pain?"

Plank Three:

Repent of your sins; stop giving yourself the right to a pity party.

That sounds kind of harsh, almost like kicking a man while he's down. But look at Job 42:6. *"Wherefore I abhor myself, and repent in dust and ashes."* When you look at the man who has lost everything- his health is gone, his wealth is gone, his family is gone- he has been basically left with the breath in his lungs, a cranky spouse, and a couple of accusing friends. After Job's conversation with God, he began to see a different picture of his life. Job was a wonderful person. I believe the scripture portrays Job as a very decent, moral, and upstanding family man. But the Bible is also clear on the subject of sin... *"There is none righteous, no, not one* (Romans 3:10)," and *"For all have sinned, and come short of the glory of God* (Romans 3:23)." Nobody is perfect.

Some friends of ours built a house. During the process, the carpenters were having some trouble. The couple was getting a little upset with the shoddy work and all the mistakes. The wife was a little more vocal about it than the husband. Finally he said, "Well, there are no perfect carpenters, and the one that was perfect…well…they crucified Him." We all have our faults, some more than others, obviously, but nobody but the Lord Jesus Christ is perfect. Job, as good as he was, still had sin and was faulty. He needed to confess to God his wayward ways.

How do we put this into practice? Say for instance, we have a couple who need help. They are having marriage problems. The man is an absolute creep. He drinks, he does drugs and he hangs out in bars until the wee hours of the night. He doesn't work as he should, he's mean to the children, and he's had multiple affairs. Paint the picture as black and bleak as you want. He's a pathetic excuse for a human being. She, on the other hand, is kind, loving, and godly. She is a beautiful flower married to a pile of manure. But both, because no one is perfect, have issues. The problems are not 50/50 or even 70/30, but maybe 95/5. We must take responsibility for our own actions - even if we are only five-percent of the problem. We are 100% responsible for our 5%. Some say, "Look, get that jerk straightened out first." They're right. If we could, that would solve a big majority of this couple's problems. But experienced counselors will tell you that normally it's the person with the smaller issues who has to make a move first. If the marriage will ever be turned around, when someone admits a fault, however small, it can start a chain reaction with the other person involved. Sometimes it works…sometimes it doesn't. But the ones who took even five percent of the share of the marriage trouble will feel better because they did what they could. Two decades from now, after the marriage has broken up, they can still look back and say, "I tried. I did what I could."

The simple fact of life is you cannot control another person whether it be a spouse, one of your older children, an employee, a parent, a brother or sister, or even a good friend. You can't control them, but you can control you. And you can take responsibility for your own life. You can take responsibility for your problems. You can take responsibility for your own sin.

Let me give you a personal illustration. Years ago, I coached high school basketball at a Christian school in Indiana. I always tried to teach the team to take responsibility for their own failures. Oftentimes teams wanted to blame someone else for their losing. I would go into the locker room after the game and hear, "The refs blew the game for us," "The other team cheated," "The fans distracted us," or "The gym was too small." Once, we played a team whose gym roof was leaking. Instead of canceling the tournament, they went ahead with the games, but during the course of the weekend, it rained. At times, water would be on the court. It would have to be wiped up every few minutes. One spot in the far corner of the court was so bad a trash can sat on the court to collect the water. We had to play around it!!

Winners and overcomers have one thing in common. They keep the ability to succeed within themselves. They don't blame the refs because they can't control them. They don't blame the fans because they can't control them. They don't blame the gym floor, with the trash can collecting water, because they can't control it either. If teams are going to win and get ahead, they have to take responsibility for their own actions. They must shoot better, work harder, practice longer, and play tougher defense. Whatever. The ability to win stays within control of the team.

We can't control other people. We can't even fully control events that take place around us. But we can control our thoughts and our actions. We can choose to act upon our feelings or not. We can take responsibility for our own mistakes and sins, even if they are small. Job was down, life had delivered him a bad hand, but God forced him to look long and hard at himself.

Yes, life is rough, but stop giving yourself the right to quit life. Stop giving yourself the right to your own pity party. Yes, mourn over the loss that has come your way. It hurts. You feel empty. There's a void there. Yes, express those feelings. Job mourned for weeks on end, but eventually, he had to stop. The alternative would have been to mourn all the way to the grave.

God doesn't want that, you don't want that and your family and friends don't want that. If it helps, take a calendar and look several weeks down the road. If need be, look several months ahead in your calendar. Mark a date. That's how long you're going to give yourself to mourn and be sad over your loss. But in the meantime, work on you. What's your sin? What are your problems? What mistakes have you made? Begin to get them right. Confess, make amends, apologize, seek forgiveness from God, or if you've hurt or wronged someone else, go talk to them. Something took place years ago, something horrible. You were abused, taken advantage of, molested or even raped. Do not let that person who took your past away also take your future away.

In May of 2009, two articles appeared in the local paper. One was of an attempted murder case. A Kentucky man with a lengthy criminal record was stalking his ex-girlfriend. He eventually took a knife and stabbed her eleven times. Before that, he had harassed her, violently assaulted her, and even chased her with his car, ramming her vehicle. Because of the attack, she also lost her unborn child. At the court hearing, she said to the judge and those in the court, but especially to her ex-boyfriend, "You have destroyed my life, both physically and mentally. I hate the scars I have left on my body." I feel so sorry for this young lady. She had been taken advantage of. She'd been unduly hurt and almost killed. The whole situation she went through was not right, but keeping a hatred and bitterness toward this man was not causing him pain. It was causing her pain. This monster stole part of her life and part of her past. It's her choice now whether he will steal part of her future.

Another article was about a killer who was on his last and final appeal to avoid the death penalty. The 34-year-old daughter of the victim was at the hearing. This man changed her life by killing her mother back in 1983. But she said this about the killer, "I am a Christian, and I am not bitter. I will not allow him to have that type of power over my life." One lady said, "I blame you for my circumstances and my life." She will ever be in a state of turmoil. The other said, "I will control my life from here on out. I can't control the awful thing you did, but I can control myself right now. I take full responsibility for my thoughts, my actions, and my life."

You're on the Island of Hopelessness. Maybe you, like Job, were taken and placed here through no fault of your own, or you made some mistakes that have landed you there. Whichever the case, the third plank you must add to your raft is taking responsibility for yourself. You must take ownership of your own mistakes that have gotten you to the place where you are. You must also take ownership for your own sin. If you're keeping a grudge against another human being, the Bible tells you in Romans 12:19, *"Dearly beloved, avenge not yourselves, but rather give place unto wrath; for it is written, vengeance is mine; I will repay, saith the Lord."* You feel justified in your anger and in your feelings of hatred toward this person who has caused you loss, but God says to leave it in His capable hands. You want to hurt them as much as they have hurt you, but God says to leave it with Him. You'll be better off in the long run. If you're holding bitterness against another, confess that sin to God and get your own heart right. I John 1:9 tells us, *"If we confess our sins, He is faithful and just to forgive us our sins and to cleanse us from all unrighteousness."* Plank Three is simple to state but very difficult to put in practice, but keep working on it. It will eventually come. "Repent of your sins.....stop giving yourself the right to a pity party."

If Paul the Apostle had not let go of his guilty past, we would not have the fourteen books of the New Testament he had wrote. After King David confessed to all the sin he had committed, God said, "He is a man after My own heart." Stop holding bitterness against someone else who has hurt you. When the Lord Jesus was on the cross, He looked at the very Roman soldiers who whipped Him with a cat of nine tails, the very soldiers who crowned Him with thorns, who spit on Him, who drove the nails into His feet and hands and said, "Father, forgive them, for they know not what they do."

Repent of your sins…stop giving yourself the right to a pity party.

Raft Building Questions:
Plank Three

1. What does the Bible say about people in Romans 3:23?
   What does the Bible say about Jesus Christ in Hebrews 5:9?

2. What do winners and over comers have in common?

3. Are you willing to take responsibility right now for your own failures, shortcomings, problems, mistakes and sin? Are you willing to write them down, confess them and take them to the cross of Jesus Christ? Are you willing to seek grace and forgiveness? If so, write them down and confess them to God.

4. What is the main lesson you take away from Plank Three?

"Is my dream dead?"

Plank Four:

React humbly. Become the servant of God.

Pray and minister to others.

"Therefore take unto you now seven bullocks and seven rams, and go to my servant Job, and offer up for yourselves a burnt offering; and my servant Job shall pray for you: for him will I accept: lest I deal with you after your folly, in that ye have not spoken of me the thing which is right, like my servant Job. So Eliphaz the Temanite and Bildad the Shuhite and Zophar the Naamathite went, and did according as the Lord commanded them: the Lord also accepted Job. And the Lord turned the captivity of Job, when he prayed for his friends.." Job 42:8-9, 10a

What is wonderful about these planks is they come straight from the Bible. I'm not making these up. I'm not giving you my own philosophy of life. I'm not even giving you the newest trend of counseling techniques. These principles come straight from the time-tested ancient scriptures. There is no fluff - just straight facts. If you truly want off the Island of Hopelessness, now it can be done. Again, it will take hard work and God's grace. Take hold of God's Word and believe His promises. Philippians 4:13 says, "I can do all things through Christ which strengtheneth me." I Corinthians 10:13 says, "There hath no temptation taken you but such as is common to man; but God is faithful, who will not suffer you to be tempted above that ye are able; but will with the temptation also make a way to escape, that ye may be able to bear it." Many people before you have journeyed off this island. They gathered their planks from God's word, tied their boat together, and set sail. Furthermore, people who land on this island after you will make it off. By implementing these basic guidelines, every castaway can make it. This book is written as a practical "rubber meets the road" manual to get you off the island. It has not been written in an ivory tower but down in the trenches where real people live and have real problems.

Plank Four may seem like the last thing in the world you want to do, but helping others is exactly what the doctor ordered. In this case, the doctor is God. At the end of God's final statement to Job and his friends, God says, "You three amigos were wrong. Seek Job out and ask him to pray for you." If we set up the scene, Job's still in misery in his torn clothes. He still has boils and blisters all over his body. He's dirty, smelly, and still covered in ashes. He's still the one who has lost everything: health, wealth, and family. He's still whimpering in pain because of the burden of grief. His eyes are red and swollen. His tears have washed streaks down his soot-blackened cheeks. And now, as if he didn't have enough on his plate, he is asked to pray for his companions.

    I heard of an old preacher who years ago gave this same advice to a middle-aged woman in his congregation. She came to him with a heavy heart. She was terribly depressed. She was miserable. She didn't even want to get out of bed in the morning. Her body ached and she was tired all the time. The old preacher listened and sized up the situation very quickly. With all the "horse sense" he could muster, he told her to go volunteer to cook food at the homeless shelter and also to begin cleaning the Sunday School rooms each week after services: wiping off desks, sweeping floors, and emptying trash. Then, he told her to take some meals and visit some of the elderly in the church who were now shut-ins. The pastor saw the woman many weeks later and asked how she was doing. He asked her if she was still depressed. The woman looked at him as if he were a crazy man: "Depressed? I don't have time to be depressed!"

It may sound strange, but you can actually work your way out of depression. Be very cautious here. Remember, there are seven planks…not one. To simply just get very busy so as to forget your misery will not do. One plank alone will probably get you out to the reef. You're only a couple hundred yards off the island. Without all seven planks, you're going to end up back on the island again. But it is true…you need to look around you and find someone else to help. In this life, we can always find someone more miserable than ourselves. Try to help them up. In Job's case, nobody was in a worse condition. He had hit the bottom of all humanity. But the principle was still the same. God, in essence, said, "Job, stop focusing only on yourself, look around you and help others." Philippians 2:4 says, *"Look not every man on his own things, but every man also on the things of others."* There is a valley the Bible talks about called the Valley of "Baca" or the Valley of "Weeping." Psalm 84:5-7 says, *"Blessed is the man whose strength is in thee; in whose heart are the ways of them. Who passing through the valley of Baca makes it a well; the rain also filleth the pools. They go from strength to strength, every one of them in Zion appeareth before God."*

At first glance these verses seem not to do a lot for us. But upon closer examination, we discover those "wells" are made with tears.

Someone has passed this hard path before. On their journey, they've stopped and cried. You're traveling down this same road. You've lost something dear to you. Your life has been turned upside down. As you stop, tears flow down your cheeks like rain. They, too, are filling up these wells. One day, somebody will come behind you. Someone you can help. They are in agony. They are in conflict of soul and spirit. They are crying out to God "Why? Why? Why?" They will receive strength from "well to well."

Use your pain and suffering unselfishly and help others, purposely making pools of refreshing water to get somebody back to God. There is always someone hurting more than you. Take time to empathize and sympathize with them. There are so many churches and organizations out there which need volunteers: Hospice, Boys and Girls Clubs, homeless shelters, food pantries, ministries to children, ministries to the newly divorced, ministries to addicts and alcoholics, ministries to widows and widowers, and ministries to the abused. This world is full of hurt. Take time to provide some healing amidst your sorrow. Some depression is compounded because you are actually too focused on yourself: my problems, my dilemmas, my feelings, my circumstances, and even my solutions. God wanted Job to minister and pray for his friends.

Benjamin Franklin once said, "When you are good to others, you are best to yourself." The great psychiatrist, Alfred Adler, used to say to his melancholy patients, "You can be cured in fourteen days if you follow this prescription. Try to think everyday how you can please someone." It is said that Dr. Karl Menninger, the famous psychiatrist, once gave a lecture on mental health and was answering questions from the audience. Someone asked, "What would you advise a person to do if that person felt a nervous breakdown coming on?" Most people thought he would say, "Go see a psychiatrist immediately," but he didn't. To their astonishment, Dr. Menninger replied, "Lock up your house, go across the railroad tracks, find somebody in need, and help that person."

One of the saddest stories I've heard in recent years is of John C. Odom. Maybe it's because I grew up playing sports, and I know the pressure athletes put on themselves, or maybe it's because I'm looking at his picture right now. He is wearing a red baseball hat with a yellow bill and a red button-down jersey. A Bronco proudly graces the front of the shirt as the team logo. This young man is smiling, and you can tell he's well-built and strong. He's just a good-looking athlete. John C. Odom pitched for the minor league baseball team, the Laredo Broncos. He didn't become famous for his skills as a pitcher, but instead for the trade of which he was a part. You see, John was traded to the Alexandria Aces of Louisiana for ten maple bats. He became a punch line, nicknamed "Bat Boy," "Batman," and "Bat Guy." During one interview, John said, "People are like, 'I'd kill myself' and stuff," but he dismissed the idea.

Three weeks later, he left the team abruptly. He was a joke for sports shows and newscasts. But within a six month time, it was no joke. John C. Odom was dead. At age 26, he accidentally overdosed on heroin, methamphetamine, the stimulant Benzylpiperazine, and alcohol. His former manager, Dan Shwam from the Broncos, said, "I really believe, knowing his background, that this drove him back to the bottle, that it put him on the road to drugs again. There were some demons chasing him. They'd been after him for a long time, but there's no way to really know whether the trade did it. Is there?"

How tragic. A young man with a bright future, snuffed out because he lost his dream. He thought maybe he could go far, but it didn't materialize. Was his life over? Why, no! But when you're in pain of heart and soul you just want relief. The drugs and alcohol briefly took him away. He could never get back on track. Had I been counseling a man like this, who just was disappointed over his career, I would have suggested volunteering.

Think for a moment with me: this young man, age 26, shows up at a little league field. A team of ten-year-old boys stand around him, and he begins to tell his stories of playing ball in the minor leagues. Can you see this young man, a semi-professional baseball player, giving instruction and encouragement to a bunch of kids? They would have thought he was the great Nolan Ryan, Randy Johnson, or Greg Maddax. He could have worked a job during the day and in the evening, coached a team. Those boys would have loved him. He would have been an instant hit with a little league team. After he got some experience, he could have moved up to helping older boys, pouring his life into others, relating to them all his good and bad experiences, teaching them the skills of baseball. He would have been a very valuable member of society. But instead the Island of Hopelessness took another victim.

So your dream died. That does not mean your life holds no value. It just means it's time to get a new dream. Start a new direction. This fourth plank says stop focusing on yourself; put your focus unselfishly on others. The Apostle Paul said in Acts 20:35, *"I have shewed you all things, how that so labouring ye ought to support the weak, and to remember the words of the Lord Jesus, how he said, It is more blessed to give than to receive."* Make a difference in someone else's life, and you'll begin feeling good about your own.

The fourth plank calls for action instead of sitting around wondering how you're going to get off of this island. You put this book down and call a church or organization right now and volunteer. Remember what God, in essence, asked Job to do: React humbly. Become the servant of God. Pray and minister to others.

Raft Building Questions:
Plank Four

1. As Job was still whimpering in pain, his face still red and swollen, still covered in ashes and tear streaked, what was he asked to do for his companions?

2. How is some depression compounded?

3. From this chapter, write the quotes from Benjamin Franklin, Alfred Adler and Dr. Karl Menninger. Can you name a neighborhood organization you could volunteer for?

4. What is the main lesson you take away from Plank Four?

"How can I go on?"

Plank Five:

Resolve to be patient. Let God be God. You never know what time or what the tide will bring in.

"And the Lord turned the captivity of Job, when he prayed for his friends: also the Lord gave Job twice as much as he had before." Job. 42:10

In the classic film "Castaway," Tom Hanks plays Chuck Noland who works for Fed Ex. At the beginning of the movie, he is ever on the go. Time is money. Money is time. Hanks is moving and shaking, his calendar is packed with appointments, making the world of business ever faster. He races from city to city around the globe. He has the world at his feet: good job, beautiful fiancée, and a bright future. But then his world crashes. Literally. His plane goes down, and he is marooned on a deserted island. Alone and with very limited resources, he attempts just simple survival. Making fire or cracking coconuts have now become daunting tasks. Talk about discouragement: Hanks is so down that at one point, he makes plans to kill himself. He just wants to end his miserable existence, but he can't even do that. Everything is totally out of his hands. Hanks gives us an example of one of our planks. Because he can do nothing about his own circumstances, he is at the mercy of the island. Toward the end of the movie, Hanks talks with a friend: "I know what I have to do now. I've got to keep breathing because tomorrow the sun will rise. Who knows what the tide could bring?"

What he was advocating in one word was "patience." Before, he always fought time. He always fought to get things done. Now, he had nothing but time. When I say patience, I mean real patience. In America, we think waiting in front of a microwave for a full minute is too much. When we wait for half an hour at a restaurant to eat, it is too long. The movie portrayed Hanks on the island for almost five years. That means days, weeks, months, and years just crept by. He could do nothing but watch the waves come in.

One of our major problems as Christians is we don't give God enough time to be God. We try to solve our problems immediately. Our depression should just go away. Our loneliness issue should be solved immediately. We should be able to pop a pill and rid ourselves of all anxieties. God does not work in a vacuum. He works with people. His greatest creation can be very stubborn at times. People have sin, feelings, emotions, desires, and passions. So when He begins to work on fellow human beings, they resist. Could God bring down His fist and smash them to smithereens? Sure. But that's not His style. What doesn't fly this year could happen next year. If not next year, maybe next decade then. Time means nothing to God.

You have a wayward spouse who has made your life miserable. You prayed about it, but God does not seem to be working. Doesn't He care? Isn't He listening? "Hey, I could use a little help down here." But He is working. But people take time to change. That new job is coming. You just have to wait seven more months. Everything will be in place. But we say, "No, no, no…I want off this island, now. I want my circumstances to change right this very minute." But as we build this raft, we must consider this plank…patience. You never know what the tide may bring in.

The last half of verse ten says, "Also the Lord gave Job twice as much as he had before." Common sense tells us these things did not happen over night. It takes time for kids to be born. Nine months exactly. So Job slowly got his life back. God moved people and circumstances back around Job to benefit him. Favor was upon him. God began to bless the seasons, so that they were productive. Year after year, life began to return to normal. You could even say it was better than it was before. But Job sat on the Island of Hopelessness watching the waves crash in, day after day; and every couple of weeks, God brought something his way. But Job had to be patient; it didn't all come at one time. Slowly, things floated to the shore that Job could use to get off the island.

The famous author and pastor, Chuck Swindoll, tells a classic story of the boll weevil. A quick internet search brings up the historic account:

In Coffee County, Alabama farmers had already been devastated by two boll weevil outbreaks. But in 1916, a local farmer hit a homerun with an experimental crop called "peanuts." The crop was perfectly suited for the sandy red soils of the region. The area had been devastated. Farmers didn't know what they were going to do. Their cotton crops were gone. The boll weevil had laid them bare. Until that point, cotton was what drove Coffee County. If the cotton crop came in well, the county did well. If there was no cotton, there was no economy. But the boll weevil had struck again. So farmers in Coffee County realized they could make more money by growing peanuts than they ever could by growing cotton. And in fact, by 1939, records showed that just a little after twenty-five years after peanuts were introduced in Coffee County, the county produced 19.6 million pounds of peanuts and only 9,100 bails of cotton. So, in December of 1919, the city erected a monument statue of the boll weevil, which had saved their lives, because if it wasn't for the destruction and the pain that the boll weevil caused, the farmers would have never discovered the crop called "peanuts." Today you can still go to Coffee County and see the statue. In fact, it's a tourist area. You can buy boll weevil t-shirts and trinkets in the gift shop.

Those farmers thought their lives were devastated. Their livelihood was over, but with time and patience they ended up better than they ever thought they would.

God has set a verse before us that at times drives us insane. It is a verse that is quoted at the most dire of circumstances. Christians know it well. Romans 8:28 says, *"And we know that all things work together for good to them that love God, to them who are the called according to His purpose."* We must let God be God. If you can right now look up to Heaven and say "God, I have loved You and I still love You," "God, I have served you and I will continue to serve you," "God, I have set my life in motion to fulfill Your purpose and I will continue to live for Your purpose," then simply trust God. He has made a promise to you. With enough time and enough waves, He will bring things to you that you can use to get off the Island of Hopelessness.

In my pastorate, I have met a lot of people. One bitter soul made an impression on me that I have not forgotten. The individual felt as if God was mistreating him. So his comment about serving God and giving to God was this, "I'll start giving to God when He starts giving to me."

We, as Christian people, are God's servants. God is not our servant. He is not a genie in a lamp for you to rub and then order around. "Hey, God, come out here and fix my circumstance. Give me this, and then I'll do this for You." That is ungodly thinking. Live for Him, serve Him, love Him, and when struggles come your way, trust Him. If you're doing those things, sit back, be patient, and watch God bring about something good in your life. Plank Five is all about patience. Attach this plank to the other four. As you listen to waves rush in, and you watch the white foam subside back into the ocean, stow this principle away in your mind and never forget it. Resolve to be patient. Let God be God. You never know what time or the tide might bring in. "Live for Him, serve Him, love Him." Step back and be patient.

Raft Building Questions:
Plank Five

1. At the beginning of this chapter/plank, what was the quote from Tom Hanks in the movie "Castaway?" What one word was he advocating?

2. How much did God give back to Job according to Job 42:10?

3. Since we need to "let God be God", what does Romans 8:28 mean to you?

4. What is the main lesson you take away from Plank Five?

"When does this cycle stop?"

Plank Six:

Receive advice and resources. Let others help you.

"Then came there unto him all his brethren, and all his sisters, and all they that had been of his acquaintance before, and did eat bread with him in his house: and they bemoaned him, and comforted him over all the evil that the Lord had brought upon him: every man also gave him a piece of money, and every one an earring of gold." Job 42:11

In the Spring of 2009, I took five Sunday morning messages and dealt with the topic of depression. After one of the services, one of our local policemen came up to me and said, "You know, this thing you're preaching on right now is so needful. Just last week in Lindenwald, I made three suicide runs. One woman overdosed on a bunch of pills, a man took a shotgun and killed himself with his family sitting in the next room, and another left a note and hanged himself."

One cop, one week, and in one area of our town of 65,000 people, three individuals felt they had no other way out of their messed up lives but to just end it. This same policeman told me a couple of weeks later that he checked with dispatch and asked how many other suicide calls they received. Just over a six month period, there were 369 attempted suicides in our city. Sixty-eight had succeeded in ending their lives. The present recession has caused many to lose hope.

Forty-one-year old David Kellermann was among those who felt the squeeze. Unfortunately, Kellermann didn't take his neighbors' advice. They told him he needed to quit his job at Freddie Mac. Kellermann was the chief financial officer. The mortgage bust and debacle of 2008-2009 caused nightmares all over the United States. Kellermann had only been at the post since September. His neighbors had noticed how much weight he had lost and that he had talked about the strain of the new job. They said he needed to avoid the stress. But he said he wanted to help the company through its problems. Kellermann worked long hours and had a tense relationship with the government oversight regulators. With loans going bust at record levels, with no end in sight, the government breathing down his neck, the company and the community, at large, depending on him to solve the problem, there was no hope. For Kellermann, there was no hope. He hanged himself in his basement.

Many men and women, in businesses both large and small, have felt that pressure. It feels like this: Everybody is looking to you. You must seek out those who owe you money, your employees need paid, the other clients are waiting for their payoff, and you're stuck in the middle. Your own family needs taken care of, but you don't know how the company is going to survive. You can't just fold it up and quit. Too many people would lose out and be hurt so you keep going, not knowing what next week will bring.

Kellermann should have let others help him. He should have heeded their advice and resigned from that position. He obviously thought he could handle it, but he couldn't. Was money really worth losing his life over? Couldn't he have just sold everything, moved to a small rural community, into a little house, got a job as a Wal-Mart greeter, and just played with the kids in the back yard?

We must keep things in perspective. So what that you're not making a six figure income. I've never seen a U-Haul following a hearse. No matter how much you make, you can't take it with you. Sometimes we have to listen to others and let them help us. That's what Job's true friends did. He was down, and they came by to do what they could. First, they ate bread with him…simply talked with him, hung out with him, fellowshipped with him. Next they bemoaned him. They just listened. They took pity on him and had sympathy for him. The best counselors are first good listeners. They let you get things off your chest. Job's friends comforted him and encouraged him and, lastly, each gave him some money and a piece of jewelry to help him get back on his feet. Sometimes you just need a helping hand. Pride will keep you from receiving it, though. I'm tough…I'll keep all my problems to myself…I'll not say anything to anybody…I'll not ask for help…I'll not take a small loan from a family member…I won't receive a neighbor's gift…I'm too good for that. Sometimes we - as frail, emotional, distraught human beings - are in no condition to climb the next mountain, and bottom line…we just need a little help.

In the summer of 1989, Mark Wellman, a paraplegic, gained national recognition by climbing the sheer granite face of El Capitan in Yosemite National Park. On the seventh and final day of his climb, the headlines of The Fresno Bee *read, "Showing a Will of Granite." Accompanying the headline was a photo of Wellman being carried on the shoulders of his climbing companion Mike Corbett. A subtitle said, "Paraplegic and partner prove no wall is too high to scale." What many people did not know is that Mike Corbett scaled the face of El Capitan three times in order to help Mark Wellman pull himself up once.*

Be sure to find the right Christian friend, pastor, Sunday School teacher, or counselor. Let me throw a word of caution to you. Job never needed help before. He hadn't spent a lot of time in the counselor's office. He never complained to his neighbor. There are some individuals who live to complain. They live in the counselor's office. They unload all their troubles weekly. When the neighbors see them coming, they run and hide. They've borrowed money from parents, brothers, sisters, uncles, aunts, and even second and third cousins. They live off the system. That's not Job. He was ever the giver, not the taker (Job. 29:2-16). Some people are continual takers. They are like leeches going from one friend to another and sucking the life out of them. They know a lot of people, but never stay close to anyone because no one can take them for very long. If that's you…stop. Turn yourself around and become a giver. Listen to people. Become a true friend. Job had always been a blessing to be around. He just ran into a rough patch. If you've run into a rough patch, let some folks help you, whether trained government professionals, hired doctors, counselors, or church-run organizations. A couple of trips to the pastor's office might be all you need. A phone call to your son or daughter might just do the trick. What have you lost? Why has this depression hit? Who can help you? Maybe telling a friend can gain you a new perspective and swing you in a new direction.

In his book, *"The Closest of Strangers,"* Dr. James Judge tells a tragic story of a janitor at a community hospital who shut everybody out and wouldn't let anybody help him. These events took place when Dr. Judge was a second-year family-practice resident. He began each day by taking some medical students from room to room and teaching them how to examine the patients. He would walk into a room, explain the situation, and his customary practice was to go and lean on the waist high heater at the side of the room and look out the window.

"I was drawn to the paint-box-blue sky. It was so clear. I wanted to step right out into it. Freedom. To have a day where I could do whatever I wanted without a hundred people's expectations. I looked out over the trees and the city and the cars below, all moving fast to somewhere I knew nothing about. Life was in full motion and it felt like I was missing it. What I didn't see as I went through this room by room ritual, was the face of a man standing at the first window in the adjacent wing, staring out much like me. Not until it was too late."

Dr. Judge and his students worked their way back down the hall and were now in a room closest to the nursing station. While the patient was being examined by the medical students, Dr. Judge heard a crash. He looked out the window and not ten feet away, at the adjacent window of the other wing, was a man frantically smashing through it with a mop bucket. Dr. Judge said the man's eyes were blazing. He looked like a mad man. The two medical students both stepped up to the window to watch the horrific scene.

"What is that man doing?" said one of the medical students in disbelief. Finally the man crashed the mop bucket through the window and began to remove the shards of glass away with his bare hands. A wave of nausea swept over Dr. Judge as he started to realize the man's intentions.

"He kept looking over his shoulder: A look of desperate horror frozen on his face. I remembered thinking it was not too much of a horror of what was ahead of him as of what was behind. There was something he was willing to pay any price to get away from. He looked terrorized, pursued: one step ahead of something monstrous. And he was doing everything in his power to escape. All in one moment, he leaned out the window, struggled over the waist high ledge, and then when he was halfway out, as if

noticing for the first time, he paused a moment and locked eyes with mine. Then arms at his side, he jumped head first.

The doctor said after that, events moved like a whirlwind. He rushed out of the room and around the elevators to the swinging doors from the room where the man had just jumped. He went to the window and looked down, and he saw the man's crumpled body six floors below. The doctor then rushed down the flights of stairs, seeking a window onto the roof where the man had landed. The medical students stayed right with Dr. Judge.

When they got down to the third floor, the doctor asked the clerk where a door or window was to get out onto the roof. No one knew of any. Finally the doctor ran into a patient's room that was near the man. The room was a scene of hysteria. Three nurses were trying to get two elderly bedridden women away as fast as they could. They had seen everything. They were watching as shards of glass had come down, a mop bucket, and then finally the man landed not three feet outside of their window. They had witnessed all of it. The only opening was a two-foot-wide transom window that tilted open just halfway. The doctor, with the help of the medical students, climbed through the window. The doctor continued to write,

"I found myself on my knees with broken glass and gravel and blood all around. The panic and screaming of a moment before was replaced with the final agonal breaths of the man at my knees and the soft distant sounds of a city going about its business, not seeming to know or care. The man's arms and legs were arranged unnaturally, his eyes opened and bulging, not seeing, his chest heaving deeply. I looked over him as best I could. It was apparent that he had landed on his head. The entire back portion of skull was soft and indented. He had done the deed. By now the medical students had also inserted the head nurse through the same window, and we knelt together over the man. "I don't think we have a lot to work with, Sherry. This guy definitely landed on his head," I said breathlessly. "He's an employee, Jim. He works here," Sherry replied. For the first time, I looked at his face. Really looked at it and immediately recognized him. He worked maintenance. Or was it nursing? For some reason I thought I remembered him in post-op with a stethoscope around his neck, taking vitals. But no, I must be wrong, because I was sure I had seen him earlier that same week at about seven or eight o'clock in the evening. He was mopping the floor. Actually, he was just leaning on the mop. He looked

up and stared at me as I passed. He didn't say anything and neither did I. I just walked by.

The doctor and the nurse continued to work for several minutes. The whole time, things were being handed through the window to try to save the man: an IV, defibrillator, paddles, and other equipment. The doctor had given the man CPR for at least twenty-five minutes. Finally, he said to the rest of the folks helping, "He's had no heart beat, no spontaneous respirations for a long time. I don't think we're going to get anywhere. I think we should call it. I don't know what we're accomplishing." The others agreed and the CPR stopped. The doctor continued his writing.

Over the next two days the hospital grapevine provided a lot more detail into the man's story. I was right about seeing him in the post-op area, but that had been several months ago. He had initially worked as a nurse's aide. He had served as a medic in Vietnam and was pursuing some kind of further training. He had a wife and two children and no big problems he had ever talked to anyone about. But it wasn't long before things started to unravel. He began to withdraw from friends and family and eventually into a shell not even his wife could penetrate. Over the months, his performance took a parallel down hill course. The nursing supervisor, trying to be protective, had gradually put him into roles of less and less responsibility. But soon it was apparent that any patient-care role was not appropriate. She had talked to the Director of Maintenance and was able to get him transferred so at least he could stay employed. His detachment only progressed. Recently he had started meeting with personnel who urged him to get some counseling. No one knew whether he had or not. Over the last several weeks, many people reported seeing him standing in the hallway at night for long stretches of time, holding onto his mop, just staring into the dark…Whatever it was, he struggled with it alone, not noticing for the most part, going unnoticed by the world around him. It was determined that he had been standing in the same position staring out that same window for almost two hours before he jumped.

For weeks and months later, Dr. Judge continued to have flashbacks. He couldn't shake the vision of the man looking straight into his eyes. The man was seeming to say as he looked at the doctor in that last moment, "Please give me a reason not to do this" or "Please don't"…It took months for the flashbacks to stop, months to stop jumping every time there was a loud noise, months to be able to walk past that service room on the eighth floor without stopping to stare and rerun the whole tape…Even as the flashbacks of that final moment began to dim, but before they did, one chilling aspect changed. "Whenever I relived that last moment, when I looked into his face, right before he jumped, it was no longer his face staring back at me. It was my own."

People who have lived on the Island of Hopelessness know what it is like to feel as if there is no solution, or there is no way out. In 2009, a local popular judge from Warren County got some bad news about his health; he was also dealing with family issues. Although he was a beloved judge in the community, he committed suicide. This is never the answer. Seek help. Somehow make your life worth living. This is the sixth plank and by adding it to the others you can get off the island. You can piece your life back together. Suicide happens to the young and old, rich and the poor, educated and uneducated, but the cause is the same...hopelessness.

Young eighteen-year-old James Dungy, son of the compassionate, soft-spoken, former football coach Tony Dungy of the Indianapolis Colts, felt he had nothing to live for when he took his life. But if he would have reached out for help, even in the last minutes, someone could have given him a new perspective on life, something worth living for.

On June 2, 2009, I.E. Millstone jumped off a bridge into the Missouri River. He was 102 years of age. He was a historic builder and philanthropist. He built dozens of St. Louis landmarks including the old

Busch stadium and fountains near Union Station. He was also a leader in the local Jewish community. Millstone should have reached out for help. He should have found something new to live for. He should have found a new project to help out on. He should have found a new angle on life. But suicide is not the answer. God, in His Word, has never condoned it. But some say, "I just can't take the pressure anymore." Seek help and a new area of life. Seek out a friend or relative. Maybe a pastor or a doctor. Go to a teacher. Go to a counselor and find something to live for.

As a Christian and pastor, I can tell you that God is worth living for. Jesus Christ came two thousand years ago to die as a sacrifice for mankind's sin. We gain access to Heaven because of Him. He gave it all so that we might have life and have it more abundantly (John 10:10). Don't throw that promise away. Maybe your life, the last several years, has been lived selfishly. Begin to focus on others. Bring God's light to someone. Bring joy to someone's life. Find that new angle on life. Put Plank Six into practice right now…Where can you find someone to help? Call them now. Seek them out this week. Job did. God put together a wonderful life for him after he had lost everything. The same can happen to you.

Raft Building Questions:
Plank Six

1. Who came to Job and what did they bring him according to Job 42:11?

2. What is it that keeps us from receiving help?

3. Why do people commit suicide? Who is worth living for?

4. What is the main lesson you take away from Plank Six?

"Why is everybody living…but me?"

Plank Seven:

Resist negativism and make a new life out of what the Lord gives you.

"So the Lord blessed the latter end of Job more than his beginning: for he had fourteen thousand sheep, and six thousand camels, and a thousand yoke of oxen, and a thousand she asses. He had also seven sons and three daughters." Job 42:12-13

Simply put, don't focus on what you don't have. Focus on what you do have. The old Christian hymn "Count Your Blessings" gives us the perfect platform for this last plank. We are only human and as human beings we love to focus on the negative. When the nightly news comes on, the lead stories notoriously are negative. We are drawn in. Our newspapers ninety-percent of the time have the latest dirt on the front page. The next time you look at your internet news, count how many stories on the screen are positive. Now, how many are negative?

Even in our personal lives, we have much difficulty avoiding negative comments.

I'll give you a perfect example to which everyone can relate. You work diligently on a project, whether it is painting a picture, building a new flowerbed, writing an article for the local paper, designing a new t-shirt logo for your bowling team, or singing a solo at church. Ten people talk to you about it. They say things like, "Your song was beautiful. That meant so much to me." "Your painting has such character and depth." "I love the new bowling team logo." "The new flower bed looks wonderful." The accolades just keep coming in. Nine out of ten people are positive. They totally appreciated your work and effort. But one says, "You could have done this better." One out of ten says, "When you sang, I heard you go off tune." "I like the old team logo better." "That picture looks like garbage. I wouldn't put it up in my garage." "Your article stunk. It looked like a two-year-old wrote it." Which person do we focus on? Which comment lingers in our mind? The negative. Why do we insist on ignoring the nine encouraging people who were honest and instead think of just the one? He, too, was honest, but why does his one opinion matter more than the others? A smart and wise businessman once told me, "Scott, don't let the negative ten percent overshadow the positive ninety percent. You're not going to please everybody all the time. Focus on the ninety percent." He was right. I was consistently focusing on the negative, trying to solve their issues, putting out their latest fire, putting more stock into their opinions than into the good-hearted, positive ninety percent. It is a trap we all have fallen into at one time or another. The same goes for our lives. We focus on the negative rather than the positive.

In this seventh plank, we are to make a new life out of what the Lord gives us. Consider Edward Roy. He is from Pompano, Florida. Talk about a negative business! Mr. Roy ran Jiffy John's Portable Toilets. He rented to folks who needed an outdoor bathroom for band concerts, construction sites, church picnics, or any outdoor gathering. Mr. Roy had negative consequences from his business. He didn't know what to do with the "stuff" after it was collected. He could have taken it to a dump site, but that would have chewed up his profits. Being an intelligent business man, he wanted to figure out a way to take the negative and turn it into a positive. As he searched for a solution, he found a solar heating process that turned sewage into fertilizer. It was a stroke of genius. Instead of trying to sell the technology to the local Florida communities, his company expanded, and he began to operate the plant itself. His company would take the sewage for a fee, convert it into fertilizer, and in turn sell that fertilizer for a substantial profit. His limited partnership soon produced the cash. Jiffy Industries, the new name, provided a good tax shelter. In fact, Newsweek Magazine reported that the Jiffy stock turned in one of the best performances on the American Stock Exchange, rising from $.92 a share to a whopping $16.50. With dozens of states suffering from huge amounts of sewage problems, Jiffy's anaerobic digester caught on everywhere. It is funny when you think about it: Edward Roy literally stopped and looked at what he had, the "stuff," and started his new company with the most awful thing.

We consistently look at our problems, the burdens of life, the curses, the failures - and we forget the blessings. The old hymn, "Count Your Blessings" says…

When upon life's billows you are tempest tossed,
When you are discouraged, thinking all is lost,
Count your many blessings, name them one by one,
And it will surprise you what the Lord hath done.
Are you ever burdened with a load of care?
Does the cross seem heavy you are called to bear?
Count your many blessings, every doubt will fly,
And you will be singing as the days go by.

When you look at others with their lands and gold,
Think that Christ has promised you His wealth untold;
Count your many blessings, money cannot buy
Your reward in heaven, nor your home on high.
So, amid the conflict, whether great or small,
Do not be discouraged, God is over all;
Count your many blessings, angels will attend,
Help and comfort give you to your journey's end.
Count your blessings, name them one by one:
Count your blessings, see what God hath done;
Count your blessings, name them one by one;
Count your many blessings, see what God hath done.

Seriously, we say, "I have no money" or "I lost my job." Okay, but look…you have a wonderful spouse and good kids. "My family is pathetic." Okay, but you have a good church family that loves you. "My health is deteriorating. Okay, but your mind is still sharp. My house just burned down." Okay, but you've still got your health. "I've lost everything." Okay, but you still have God. The parable of the pearl of great price may not seem to make sense, but when you look at it with salvation in mind, the light bulb in your brain should click on. "Ahhh, now I get it." Matthew 13:45-46 says, *"Again, the kingdom of heaven is like unto a merchant man, seeking goodly pearls. Who, when he had found one pearl of great price, went and sold all that he had, and bought it."* I mean, he sold everything to gain that one pearl. In a physical material world, it is not wise, but in a spiritual sense, God must mean everything to you. If you are only left with Him and Him alone, you can be happy. But as Americans, we are spoiled by the comforts of life, and we take them for granted. Our car breaks down; it costs us seventy-five dollars to have it towed to the mechanic, it will cost another three-hundred dollars to get it fixed. Our second car is a piece of junk, a Gremlin that smells like cats. We gripe and belly-ache, but the vast majority of the population of Planet Earth doesn't even have a car.

Job lost literally everything, but he never lost his faith. So he built on that. Next came some good friends who brought guidance, friendship, and resources. So he built on that. He still didn't have much, but for what he did have, he was thankful for. Then came his first camel. Remember, he used to have three thousand. But he became thankful for the one. Why focus on the negative? Why focus on the three thousand he used to have? Then came the first sheep, then the first ox. The next camel came along. Then the first child was born. Job couldn't have stopped his children from being slain. There was nothing he could do about it, but now God was giving him a new life. Slowly, things were turning around. But you have five camels in the pen when you used to have thousands upon thousands upon thousands; so many that they were kept on multiple properties. Now all your flock sits in your back yard huddled together, all ten eyes staring at you. What a difference. But we must be thankful for what we do have, not what we don't.

In his book, *How To Stop Worrying And Start Living*, Dale Carnegie tells an incredible story about a woman by the name of Borghild Dahl. Mrs. Dahl wrote a book entitled *I Wanted To See*. Carnegie says,

> *"This book was written by a woman who was practically blind for half a century. "I had only one eye," she writes, "and it was so covered with dense scars that I had to do all my seeing through one small opening in the left of my eye. I could see a book only by holding it up close to my face and straining my one eye as hard as I could to the left." But she refused to be pitied, refused to be considered "different." As a child, she wanted to play hopscotch with other children, but she couldn't see the markings. So after the other children had gone home, she got down on the ground and crawled along with her eyes near to the*

marks. She memorized every bit of the ground where she and her friends played and soon became an expert at running games. She did her reading at home, holding a book of large print so close to her eyes that her eyelashes brushed against the pages."

She earned two college degrees, an A.B. from the University of Minnesota and a Masters of Arts from Columbia University. She started teaching in the tiny village of Twin Valley, Minnesota, and rose until she became a professor of journalism and literature at Augustana College in Sioux Falls, South Dakota. She taught there for thirteen years, lecturing before Women's Clubs and giving radio talks about books and authors. "In the back of my mind," she writes, "there had always lurked a fear of total blindness. In order to overcome this, I adopted a cheerful almost hilarious attitude toward life." Then in 1943, when she was fifty-two years old, a miracle happened: An operation at the famous Mayo Clinic. She could now see forty times as well as she ever had been able to before. A new and exciting world of loveliness opened before her. She now found it thrilling even to wash dishes in her kitchen sink. "I began to play with the white fluffy suds in the dish pan," she writes. "I dip my hands into them and I pick up a ball of tiny soap bubbles. I hold them up against the light, and in each of them I can see the brilliant colors of a miniature rainbow." As she looked through the window above the kitchen sink, she saw *"the flapping gray black wings of sparrows flying through the thick, falling snow."* She found such ecstasy looking at the soap bubbles and sparrows that she closed her book with these words: *"Dear Lord, I whispered, Our Father in Heaven, I thank Thee. I thank Thee."*

Mrs. Dahl can certainly teach all of us a lesson. Instead of being depressed over her lack of eyesight, she simply enjoyed what she had, and then amazingly God gave her more.

This last plank can be added to your raft right now. Take an inventory right now of what God has given you. Begin to count your blessings. What can you be thankful for? Write it on a sheet of paper or on the back page of this book. Take stock. What do you have? Materially, what do you possess? Write them all down. Now what family members do you have? Who are your friends? Write each one down by name. What skills and talents do you have? At what are you good? List each ability. What accomplishments have you achieved, whether graduating from high school or getting a past promotion?

Finally what does God mean to you? List His various titles. What is He to you?

Are you starting to feel better? If not, there are a couple of reasons: One, you did not write them down or two, you quickly scratched down two or three things on the paper. There is more to it when you begin to diligently list everything from health to God. You'll cover the whole page.

Depression is caused by a loss of something. Face the facts: Yes, you've lost something near and dear to you. That can't be helped. You've lost your business, you've lost your home, you've lost your spouse, you've lost another family member, you've lost your health, you've lost your innocence, and you've lost your dream. Whatever you've lost, face that fact. Now look at what you do have. Look at the potential. What can God do with you? Look at the positive. Let us build on that. Let us allow God to give us a new life. One camel at a time.

One of the greatest examples of looking forward and being thankful for what we have is the Apostle Paul. In fact, he wrote a couple of verses that just jump off the pages of the Bible. Philippians 4:11 says, *"Not that I speak in respect of want: for I have learned, in whatsoever state I am, therewith to be content."* Philippians 4:4 says, *"Rejoice in the*

Lord alway: and again I say, Rejoice." I Thessalonians 5:18 says, *"In everything give thanks: for this is the will of God in Christ Jesus concerning you."* Philippians 3:13b says, *"...forgetting those things which are behind, and reaching forth unto those things which are before."* This means a lot coming from a guy who had a guilty past. He killed Christians. This comes from a man who had been bitten by a poisonous snake, who had been stoned literally to death and thrown out of the city like a piece of trash, who faced threats by a group of fanatical Pharisees who made a death pact to kill him, who perhaps was going blind, and who was in chains under house arrest as he penned these words while awaiting possible execution. His past was rough, his present was a bear, and his future was not so bright, and yet he says, "I'm content, I'm rejoicing, I'm thankful, and I'm moving forward." How could he even think like this? Because God had control of his life. He knew his Lord loved him and had died for him. He had called him for a purpose and would not leave his side.

In the Spring of 2009, a remarkable woman passed away. Her name was Martha Mason. Martha was remarkable in that during her lifetime she graduated from college at the top of her class. She also went on to graduate with honors from Wake Forest University. She entertained many folks over the years at her home. She conducted dozens of interviews and authored a couple of books. A documentary was even made about her. In the last several years, she went online, she e-mailed people, and she even set up her own Facebook account.

Now none of that seems extraordinary, except when you view all of it with the understanding that Martha Mason contracted polio in 1948 when she was eleven. The disease had killed her brother, and it crippled Martha. She was paralyzed from the neck down for sixty-one years. She spent over six decades in a horizontal world: a seven-foot long, eight-hundred pound iron lung that encased all of her body except for her head.

In an interview in 2003, she said that she chose to remain in the iron lung for the freedom it gave her. It let her breathe without tubes in her throat, incisions, or hospital stays. As newer, smaller ventilators might require, her machine took no professional training to operate, letting her remain the mistress of her own house, with just two aides assisting her. Mason went on to say, "I'm happy with who I am, where I am. I wouldn't have chosen this life, certainly. But given this life, I've probably had the best situation anyone could ask for." Ever since a young age, she had refused to be defined by her physical state. She said, "I'm what goes on inside of my head." Her tenacity is seen in how she graduated not only from high school but college. She stayed in the faculty apartments with her parents, and she would listen to the lectures through the intercom system while her mother took notes. When Martha had to write a paper, she would write the paper in her head and then ask her mother to take dictation. She was a straight A student. In 2003, she produced her memoir: *"Breath: Life In The Rhythm Of An Iron Lung."* People would comment after getting to know her that, "You really begin to forget she is in an iron lung. She is so pleasant." And that's exactly how Martha wanted it: for you to treat her as an individual. People came to see her because they wanted to see her.

If anyone was tempted to be bitter, I believe it was Martha Mason. But she refused. Take a look at your own circumstances. What are you going through? Why do you feel like a castaway? Why are you isolated? Why are you depressed? Why are you lonely? Then compare yourself to a woman who was paralyzed from her neck down and spent sixty years in an iron lung. Can you honestly say that you don't have something about which to be happy? Stop focusing on what you don't have, or what you used to have, and make a new life out of what you *do* have—what God has given you today.

Not only should we resist negativism, but we should "renew our minds." The Bible is very clear on this point. As we put off our old lifestyle, old habits, old character, old desires, old thoughts and what the Bible describes as our "old man", we are to put on the "new man" and "be renewed in our minds" –renewed not with just random positive thoughts, but with God's Word.

"If so be that ye have heard him, and have been taught by him, as the truth is in Jesus: that ye put off concerning the former conversation the old man, which is corrupt according to the deceitful lusts; and be renewed in the spirit of your mind; and that ye put on the new man, which after God is created in righteousness and true holiness."-Ephesians 4:21-24

"Let the word of Christ dwell in you richly in all wisdom; teaching and admonishing one another in psalms and hymns and spiritual songs, singing with grace in your hearts to the Lord. And whatsoever ye do in word or deed, do all in the name of the Lord Jesus, giving thanks to God and the Father by him." -Colossians 3:16-17

"I beseech you therefore, brethren, by the mercies of God, that ye present your bodies a living sacrifice, holy, acceptable unto God, which is your reasonable service. And be not conformed to this world: but be ye transformed by the renewing of your mind, that ye may prove what is that good, and acceptable, and perfect, will of God." -Romans 12:1-2

Renewing our minds does not come easily. We often slip back to our old ways without even realizing it. Training ourselves to think the way God wants us to think takes determination. We must purposely take time to memorize and meditate on God's Holy Scriptures. The only way to truly change our "thoughts, beliefs, desires, and wants" is to replace them with the Word of God. One counselor I know who has helped many hurting souls says that she trains her counselees to examine their thoughts and desires in the light of eight criteria found in Philippians 4:6-9, *"Be careful for nothing: but in every thing by prayer and supplications with thanksgiving let your requests be made known unto God. And the peace of God, which passeth all understanding, shall keep your hearts and minds through Christ Jesus.* <u>*Finally, brethren, whatsoever things are true, whatsoever things are honest, whatsoever things are just, whatsoever things are pure, whatsoever things are lovely, whatsoever things are of good report; if there be any virtue, and if there be any praise, think on these things.*</u> *Those things, which ye have both learned, and received, and heard, and seen in me, do: and the God of peace shall be with you."* Notice in the underlined verse eight the filter God gives us with which to sift our thoughts. By allowing those eight criteria to control our thoughts, we will have no problem with renewing our minds. In simple terms, if what I'm thinking about is not "true," I throw it out of my mind. If what I'm thinking is not "honest," I've got to get rid of it. If it's not "just," "pure," or "lovely," my mind is not to linger on it. If that thought is not of "good report" or of "any virtue" or is not "praise worthy," I am going to kick it out of my head. But just getting the bad or negative thoughts out is not good enough. Now we must renew our minds. Memorize passages of scripture. Personalize them. Meditate on them. By replacing those negative thoughts, you will be changing from the inside out. Outward change oftentimes is only temporary but following these principles could be a turning point in your life.

We now come to the conclusion of the book. As already stated in the introduction, the Lord Jesus Christ asked the crippled man "Wilt thou be made whole?" What an absolutely ridiculous question. Who wouldn't want to be made better? On the surface, that seems like a dumb question. But as the second member of the Trinity, the Lord Jesus knows that some of us don't want to get better. We like our misery. We like the attention it brings. We like to have our excuses of why we aren't succeeding in life. So the question now comes straight at you: "Wilt thou be made whole?" If you're tired of being depressed, if you're tired of not looking forward to getting up in the morning, and tired of walking around in a hopeless gloom, it's time to get to work. Begin to pray even now, "God help me get out of this funk I'm in. God help me to get off this island of isolation, loneliness, anxiety, and depression." For years

I've used the example that two men come to a mountain. Both want to reach the top. Both pray and ask God to help them get there. One man begins to climb. The other sits down on the ground. Who do you think is going to get there first?

You've now read a complete plan about how to escape the Island of Hopelessness. The choice is yours. Get up right now, dust the sand off, leave the beach, and go get your first piece of wood.

Plank One: <u>Recognize</u> that you don't know everything.

Plank Two: <u>Relax</u> and choose to believe that God knows everything, and He can do anything.

Plank Three: <u>Repent</u> of your sins; stop giving yourself the right to a pity party.

Plank Four: <u>React</u> humbly. Become the servant of God. Pray and minister to others.

Plank Five: <u>Resolve</u> to be patient and let God be God. You never know what time or what the tide will bring in.

Plank Six: <u>Receive</u> advice and resources. Let others help you.

Plank Seven: <u>Resist</u> negativism. Make a new life out of what the Lord gives you.

Take these first steps: push off from the shore and start your voyage back home. With God, you can do this. God bless you on your journey back to Him and to an enjoyable life.

Raft Building Questions:
Plank Seven

1. Write down how God has been good to you and how He has blessed you. Begin now to list off at least five things you are thankful for?

2. What is it that you are brooding over? What is it that you feel is missing in your life? Depression is caused by a loss of something…what is it that you have lost?

3. The Lord Jesus is looking at you right now and He is asking you the questions, "Wilt thou be made whole?" Will you put these seven planks together and get off the island?

4. What is the main lesson you take away from Plank Seven?

AFTERWORD

Job survived one of the most horrific shipwrecks of all time, but we must remember that he did it with God's help. If you have never accepted Christ into your life, I'd like to take a moment and show you how. The amazing thing about God is that He loves us and tries desperately to rescue us where we are, even when we are in the deepest muck and mire of life. The Bible proves this over and over again. *"For when we were yet without strength, in due time Christ died for the ungodly."* (Romans 5:6) *"For God so loved the world, that He gave His only begotten Son, that whosoever believeth in Him should not perish, but have everlasting life."* (John 3:16)

God has given each of us gifts. Your life is a precious gift. From the very beginning of time, God created man to make choices: to choose the Tree of Life or the Tree of Knowledge of Good and Evil. He has never forced Himself upon us. God has never forced us to make the right choice or even the healthy choice. He is God, and He is a gentleman. He does not go where He is not wanted. He created us for friendship. He wants to be in your life, but He will not come in if not asked. *"Behold, I stand at the door, and knock: if any man hear my voice, and open the door, I will come in to him, and will sup with him, and he with me."* (Revelation 3:20)

God has given us the ultimate gift of salvation. It is free of charge. He paid the price of judgment on the cross, dying for you and me. It is a free gift we cannot earn. We can only receive it. *"For by grace are you saved through faith; and that not of yourselves: it is the gift of God. Not of works, lest any man should boast."* (Ephesians 2:8-9) *"For the wages of sin is death; but the gift of God is eternal life through Jesus Christ our Lord."* (Romans 6:23)

God knows that we are all different in age, intelligence, skin color, whether rich or poor-and He has a salvation plan that can cover us all. *"For whosoever shall call upon the name of the Lord shall be saved."* (Romans 10:13)

This is the promise that He gives to you… Offer up a prayer and invite Him into your life. The best piece of advice that I can give to you is to accept Jesus Christ as your Savior.

God bless,

A. Scott Miller

ENDNOTES

Introduction

1. Charles Brown, *The Landmark Anchor*, August 2008.

Chapter 2

1. James Dobson, *When God Doesn't Make Sense,* (Tyndale House Publishers, Inc. 1993), p. 125-127.

Chapter 4

1. Craig Brian Larson, *Contemporary Illustrations for Preachers, Teachers & Writers,* (Baker Books, 1996), pg. 36.
2. Dale Carnegie, *How to Stop Worrying and Start Living,* (Pocket Books, 1944) pg. 173, 181.

Chapter 6

1. Craig Brian Larson, *"Contemporary Illustrations for Preachers, Teachers & Writers,* (Baker Books, 1996), pg.
2. James Judge, M.D., *The Closest of Strangers,* (Word Publishing, 2000), pg. 34-38.
3. *The Fresno Bee, Showing a Will of Granite*, Mark Wellman, 1989.

Chapter 7

1. Craig Brian Larson, *"Contemporary Illustrations for Preachers, Teachers & Writers,* (Baker Books, 1996), pg

2. Dale Carnegie, *How to Stop Worrying and Start Living,* (Pocket Books, 1944) pg. 150-151.

3. Johnson Oatman, Jr., *Count Your Many Blessings, Baptist Hymnal,* pg. 318.